Antidote for Night

Winner, 2015 Isabella Gardner Poetry Award

ANTIDOTE
FOR NIGHT
MARSHA DE LA O
POEMS

AMERICAN POETS CONTINUUM SERIES, NO. 151

BOA EDITIONS, LTD. ROCHESTER, NY 2015

First Edition
15 16 17 18   7 6 5 4 3 2 1

For information about permission to reuse any material from this book please contact
The Permissions Company at www.permissionscompany.com or e-mail permdude@
eclipse.net.

Publications by BOA Editions, Ltd.—a not-for-profit corporation
under section 501 (c) (3) of the United States Internal Revenue
Code—are made possible with funds from a variety of sources,
including public funds from the New York State Council on the
Arts, a state agency; the Literature Program of the National En-
dowment for the Arts; the County of Monroe, NY; the Lannan
Foundation for support of the Lannan Translations Selection Se-
ries; the Mary S. Mulligan Charitable Trust; the Rochester Area
Community Foundation; the Arts & Cultural Council for Greater
Rochester; the Steeple-Jack Fund; the Ames-Amzalak Memorial
Trust in memory of Henry Ames, Semon Amzalak and Dan Amzal-
ak; and contributions from many individuals nationwide. See
Colophon on page 88 for special individual acknowledgments.

ART WORKS.
arts.gov

State of the Arts

NYSCA

Cover Design: Sandy Knight
Interior Design and Composition: Richard Foerster
Manufacturing: McNaughton & Gunn
BOA Logo: Mirko

Library of Congress Cataloging-in-Publication Data

De la O, Marsha.
  [Poems. Selections]
  Antidote for night : poems / Marsha de la O.
     pages cm. — (American poets continuum series ; no. 151)
  "Winner, 2015 Isabella Gardner Poetry Award."
  ISBN 978-1-938160-81-3 (pbk. : alk. paper) — ISBN 978-1-938160-82-0 (e-book)
  I. Title.
  PS3604.E12265A6 2015
  811'.6—dc23
                        2015019570

BOA Editions, Ltd.
250 North Goodman Street, Suite 306
Rochester, NY 14607
www.boaeditions.org
A. Poulin, Jr., Founder (1938–1996)

for corvids everywhere,
and the women who journey with them

Contents

ONE

Moon with Text

And when I heft a tomato
in my hand, sere orange, seamed
with scar along the split, in September
the bush still blossoming but fruit
no longer sets—
what's left is the last of the season. Then
the call comes, and more images needed.
Now I settle, alone, attendant gone
in search of the radiologist
but the room's not empty
a mist of souls in here, shell dust of
women who sat in the same wicker, one thing
in common—we all make this journey
with a load of sticks and knobs. Text:
"I saw the new moon late yestreen / with the old moon
in her arms / and if we go to sea, Master / I fear
we'll come to harm"   I remember pointing
at the blood moon and he folded my hand into his
Doesn't look like blood to me, more like
a flower, say, squash blossom . . . and I say it now
squash blossom, glass of water, rabbit-face
moon, where are you?   In a strange way, she's here,
they named the new machine Selene, and the hum
of her meditation never ends, Selene building
a pillar of sound, Selene, our former Tartar Queen,
Sister, Lantern, broad-shouldered Wahine.
The pale apples are lifted and pressed
onto Selene's plate. All   she sings
radiant flash   luster   joule
heat   she sings   opal   shimmer
three millimeters   she sings
at twelve o'clock

Once

That old train whistle wakes me
     at midnight, tracks hardly used
now, just a spur to the warehouse
     where they heap the cars
with lemons bound for Asia.
     Another lone cry at one,
and the train rumbles off
     to the port. Once a mockingbird
perched in the umbrella tree
     woke me, song like dark honey,
like the rain we yearn for, a cistern
     in my heart full as never again.

Passing Hyperion

1

The car lurches forward on the 101, red snake
traffic through downtown. My father
doesn't drive anymore, but he conjured this city,
my labyrinth, our treasure—this is his town.
A few neon signs blink on, each a glyph
of light, and we're in the early dark
November, 1960. He's at the wheel
driving east, me riding shotgun, truck
unloaded in Cudahy, Commerce, Norwalk,
one more stop in Boyle Heights, and cruise
the Golden State all the way home.
Huggy Boy on the radio, darkness settling
over the Marlboro Man lifting a cigarette
to his handsome lips, over Jesus Saves
across an entire rooftop, each letter blazing,
Time to Bowl in aqua, Carlin Room in flowing
gold, the Four-level Interchange coming up,
Smart Women Cook with Gas, Manny, Moe, or
Jack stands tall, heavy curved Aladdin brow,
muscles bulging from his polo—never could
tell the Pep Boys apart—our fools' paradise all
around us, red-winged horse over the Mobil
station, Wiltern Theater green as sea glass,
spotlights angling off like egrets. My father's
hands, work-thickened, curve the wheel,
scattering of dark hair across the back
of his palms, thumbnail bruised black,
salt tang of sweat—the way I love the world
is not separate from the way I love my father,
not separate from darkness sifting down,
nightdust tingeing what's left of the sky.

2

Father you no longer drive and we'll be
passing Hyperion soon. Do you remember?
We're trying to read every message
written in light—a mermaid in a martini
glass, a boy king, two cherries on a single
stem spelled out in cylinders of fire,
and these lights prove us, crawling home
through Silverlake, waiting for our favorite—
rats running the wall of *Western Exterminators*.

Death is a blind man in a top coat
hefting a sledgehammer, mallet descending,
but rats are pure mystery, offering themselves,
bright knowing eyes, flick of pink noses—
the hammer falls. Of endless rats, the world
is made, each one a fragment light passes
through, kindling form to form, dying,
dead, gone—and back in the dream
running again before we know it.
We take it all in and drive on.

Chinese Lantern

There was only one place we ever ate Chinese,
Lin's on Los Feliz,

my grandfather ruling the table
with the same almond chicken, egg foo yong,

little saucers of hot mustard. In the ceiling
they'd mounted a Chinese lantern with red tassels,

a kind of three-story castle clinging upside down
to the roof of heaven.

Depending where we sat, my sisters and I could watch lit scenes
in each castle wall—a maiden crossing a footbridge,

peach trees in blossom, two birds
on a branch leaning toward each other,

a river tumbling like raw silk through a gorge.
I always wanted to watch the birds, wanted

only the maroon booth in the back, not the ebony chairs,
and so did my cousin Diana who wore plum-colored

lipstick and teased her hair—*they're love doves,*
she whispered from the high throne of high school,

ginger and garlic rousing my mouth. The next time
we saw her there, months later, Diana was sway-backed

and swag-bellied, her eyes sad and defiant at once,
hand pressed to the small of her back, a silver moon

pendant shining between mountains of bosom.
She watched the lovebirds and didn't say anything.

I can see it now, my mother's face
twisting a wind that scatters all words,

Diana's wet eyes and the birds leaning in,
quiet after the tumult of love.

That night I felt a bird enter and sink down
through me, the bird that is thirst,

the bird that could drink an ocean and not be quenched,
because thirst is both wanting and water

and water doesn't want to stop,
water wants to let it happen

the way Diana let it happen, deliberately,
one step after another crossing a bridge,

her eyes glassy with knowledge and so quiet afterwards,
I saw what she'd been looking at all that time,

the wings of two birds going so fast—
a blur of stillness,

water roaring through a gorge
each droplet's great quiet flight

silence,
like when your mother calls out,

her voice dark with suspicion,
what are you doing in there

and you answer   *nothing*

Nobody Knows

We had to imagine you even then, Ramon, your star lost,
a glimpse to die for,
all the kids galloping to Westside Park
where your gang was supposed to meet in open warfare
those bitter skinny boys from Toonerville,
well-armed, Lupe said.
And when we got there, nothing, no armies, no chucos
with long tails and zip guns, just the grass
with its stunned look, as though it never really wanted all that light.
City grass doesn't want much of anything,
it's not out there trembling with desire,
minds its own business, leeching slowly upward from busted pipe.
And now nobody knows what you really wanted, Ramon,
when the needle spun true north,
or why that final rush of light, flat stare of lawn
as you staggered by, seared your throat shut.
Tonight, I'm getting to the smallest place I know,
dusk coming on slow,
the moon half full of shade,
so still it almost doesn't want to move,
whispers a phrase to particles of blue.
Same moon you knew with its white mind watching,
same moon you walked beneath and were gone.

Viento

Did I mention I'm afraid of the dark?
        The wind too: *Vientophobia,*
   my doctor calls it. Sets me on edge.

       All the little hairs on my forearms
           trilling upward. That night
 a gale swept through, and a honey bee

         buzzed free, lumbering in my kitchen,

wind-rocked darkness, the bee must have
         been whistled down and scrabbled
through the fan housing.

       She rose by instinct, an older
          female sent out to forage
in the fields of the realm, I like to say—

         always wished I was one of them,

old-woman-ecstatic lipping goblets
         on the trumpet vine,
the bee is rising toward stovelight

       when her thorax touches the flood—
         living flesh against diode sizzles
down hard, thrown to the floor by force,

        no telling if light ate the filaments

of her wings, still carrying treasure for the hive,
        oro blando, velvety damp
morsels of pollen. *And where art thou now,*

O Queen? Somewhere close by, bringing forth
eggs? Male and female she makes
them, opens the ductile to her sac of sperm,

fertile and infertile she forms them

in their golden cells. And her daughters shape the waxen
cakes, her sisters build the combs,
and the old ones beat their wings and tremble

in the fields. Now the night careens
toward me in the gyre of the wind,
now the stunned elder sister is laid on alien ground,

your servant, Majesty, alone in the dark

Possum

And if I made a bad meal, if leftovers,
my husband bent to scrape them into the bowl,
summoning our hound for the favor
of her indiscriminate desire,
his brows scowling together, yes, I'd open the back door
into the garage just to let the rancor out, the dog
stood in for me, her mad panicked barking.
I was pregnant, thick with it, thought to
become a woman finally, not that stick,
that boy I'd always been—instead,
a heavy figure forever wrong at dinner.
He didn't want to be a father.
And yes, I witnessed the improbable nest
a stranger's long labor, boogie board gnawed
to snowdrops lining the far corner.
We came face to face—rich silver of her ruff,
long pink tail sprouting wiry hairs like a woman's bristled chin,
a quick palsy ran through her shoulders—*discovered*—
the possum must have known it then—her ruin.
She met my gaze, lifting her plush and fragile nose.
Against my belly wall three rivers fed the blue placenta,
little matter moored by cable coiled in that water.
She stood her ground, lips drawn back,
teeth bared. Don't tell me what love endures
or need requires, don't tell me animals can't make
mortal calculation. I knew she was carrying too,
building bits of flesh that fall into the world,
thirteen teats for a litter of two dozen
infants the size of honey bees scrabbling for the pouch,
and if half of what we sow is strewn on barren ground—
scorched, choked, devoured by birds—still,
all must be borne.

Biscuit, Ingot, Spirit

As a pine marten might   wide-eyed
     as a mummer   in a jumble of vermilion
          may make   from this world   a muckle
of marvel   You   creature   from your private   lagoon
          your own   interior sea noisy pump   sluice of liquid
transparency you remember   and don't   your mouth
     forming its O   your buttermilk skin
          with   its blue map of rivers
        this shock wave   this warm-milk fall
bedaubed and stippled   with jewels   oh jolt
          of recognition   thunderbolt   as unseen hands
lift you to your element   —astonished water—
          both home and not   exiled   wonder-
struck   sound the air   every hair   alive

Sanchez

I don't recall how dark or gold his eyes were. I remember
    a darkness that might
not have been iris, something that put me in mind of my dog,
    his grateful look

and underneath, a well of grief. Maybe not his eyes, more
    the way he bore pain
with dumbfounded dignity, his trouser leg going black with blood,
    and Sanchez quiet

and far away as it ran freely down his leg, the fastest
    blood in class.
What he really knew how to do was run with those long
    rangy legs as silence

seemed to buoy him some way around the track, lap after
    lap, never changing pace.
Sanchez could go on as others fell away as though he kept the world
    within, spinning, gravity-flung

on the inside turn, while I, his teacher, labored at the last, the dead
    end of my fourth grade
class, heaving and panting as they all galloped past with the
    authority of the swift.

In class he'd lay his head sideways on the desk to write his journal
    in a wavering line, words leaning
every which way like a row of shacks in a labor camp,
    without punctuation

because the story never ended. He came from people who could run,
    his mother ran away
to Oakland with his rawboned little sister when his uncle applied
    the last of the pressure

that turned the hinge on the family door—his mother ran through it
    for a midnight bus out of town.
Sanchez was left behind, he understood why his mother had to
    take his sister and go—

she had no choice—and he knew there was nothing
    his father could do—
locked up at Rose Valley. I wanted to tell Sanchez only the best
    ones go to prison there—

addicts prone to beauty set down in a backcountry clutch
    of Quonset huts crouched
beneath their discourse with the wind. Rose Valley didn't
    bother with prison walls,

a six-foot cyclone fence was all there was, each link crying
    go if you want to,
but nobody did. That boy never wept at any injury except the time
    I kept him after school.

I don't remember the offence. Sanchez bowed his head slightly,
    tears squeezed out sideways
against his will. His eyes were a kind of glassy topaz. *Sanchez,*
    everyone makes mistakes,

and I've obviously made one here. So why don't you just go.
    He left without a word.
The boys who told me were former students back for a visit
    before graduation.

They said: *Sanchez? He's been dead more than two years.*
    Drive-by.
I didn't want to break down. I wanted to take it coolly,
    the way they'd dished it out.

I turned away and checked the clock. He always said
    he lapped me five times

and I answered *four* just to keep the argument alive,
  to see him smile and insist.

Part of me believes he's living still, loping somewhere,
  with that big slow-mo
stride, as if there were two worlds, as if the only thing left
  to do in this one is run.

Another Woman

vacuuming chrome and shadow, hot
air blowing, resting on one knee to extend
the long neck beneath the settee while
it sucks and roars and lurches across the shag
in its hopeless lumbering way, long whipcord
tail curving behind. I look at my face
in the window thinking *so this is how*
she looks cleaning house. The air is a white
fist. We all breathe open-mouthed, our chests
rise and fall like dogs. I'm the same
inside and out, all the pixels behind my eyes
making test patterns. I don't remember
when my voice took on its bitterness,
maybe it was the frozen juice in plastic
pitchers, little green oranges giving Florida
the lie. One morning it was there.
Strange how much silence can fit inside
a roar. And the nuzzle of this yearning
in my palm licking my hand. I can
see it now in the raveled threads
the spiders float off the walls, on-screen
the moisture sheen on the upper lip
of the kidnapped girl, the last one left
on the bus with terrorists. What an effort
the vacuum makes to take it in, straining
to ingest sand and dog hair, fishing
line and bits of paper that flutter off
the ends of straws, the anger in the bed
clothes and rough cotton towels. I hear
it faintly all the time, even when it's turned
off. In the morning when the first birds
carol Sunday school hymns and the mocker
does his take on the robin, it starts up, dull
and droning at another level like another

woman with veined legs in another
house who can't stop running the vacuum
with all its subtle attachments.

What It Takes

For Ernesto Garcia 1967–1995

And I have to wonder what life means since that day I heard
    Ernesto scrambled
out of the locked ward on Hillmont the same afternoon a distressed
       bear
    lumbered into the warren

of little houses off The Avenue, deputies chasing him, a three-hundred
    pound infant padding
toward mistaken water. It was one of those mornings a fat pale moon
       still
    rolls in the turquoise

and a woman stoops to pick up the *Star*, early edition—*Scientist
    awakens
    bacteria in gut of bee
doomed in amber eons ago* . . . And next to that, another story—Ernesto
    in the last shape ever

burned into anyone's eye, a shot his buddy snapped, not grasping
    it was final.
Ernesto knew not to smile for the birdie, to look past the apparatus to
    a place
    where words trail off

in a tangle of fireweed and sumac, all that grief where nothing human
    holds.
    Sundown, a big dark man
barefoot in a hospital gown, cornered up past the parking lot, copter
    thumping overhead,

shouting through tears *What am I supposed to do* until it became
    the moan rumbling
through a bear in his sleep . . . He crumpled when the gun fired, his
        mouth
    filling with nothing.

I keep seeing him make for the hills behind the mental ward, bare feet
    sliding on bits of quartz
around islands of cactus—running the shadow pulse of an older
        world—
    his stare

clean and dangerous in the scrub laurel. Three hours inside city limits
    before they hit the bear
with a tranq dart—he crumpled when the gun fired,
    unconscious—

they winched him in a sling and trucked him deep into the wild.
        Maybe that
    bear's alive, dreaming
in his bones or shambling through the understory, one huge paw
    shoveling for grubs,

light snowing the way it does at those altitudes around his dark head,
    maybe he's snuffling
air, learning to savor wind, beginning to taste what it takes to go on,
    what life wants . . .

Same Loom

Thirty-eight years working the same loom,
shuttle laying down darkness
                                    wound onto a quill.

All my chords are broken and I don't believe in God.

Small wedge of her face, eyes upturned,
Mommy, can't you be happy?
                                    Grief never stays in its bed,
bides its time and floods the valley.

I want to get it right,
                    forming words
into her serious gaze,
yes, oh yes, I'm always happy when you sing . . .
and she nods
            and disappears into the choir,

in this church we've never seen before
with its Modigliani Virgin in a pale green apse,
                            long stalk of her body.

Dark trousers or skirts, white shirts drawing in the light,
tick of anticipation   ripple of sound
and she is small among the others, and her voice tentative.

. . . happy when you sing

Behind her, that gawky green pillar, goddess-cypress
with a narrow face and verdigris eyes.

Oh green, lay on your thousand hands,
Mother of Chlorophyll,
                    Lady of Viridescence,

shelter me under the quick shimmer
                            of your silver-tipped olive.
From this river of grief, deliver me.
Let me take care of my child.

TWO

To Go to Riverside

Picture a boy,
    a smooth stone cupped in his hand—
  he's the boy David, or maybe it's a gun

    flat against his palm, and he's an archangel
    aiming for the darkened windows
  of the church. First the blast, then the shattering,

    the slap of running feet,

he never turned to see the windows fall,
    falling inside solder lines, inside lead lines
  unless the caliber was small and only

    left a bunghole of white light.
    It could have happened that way. That's why
  my father went to Riverside to make repairs

    because a saint shattered

a woman kneeling with oils or a man reaching
    for the wounds, the five glorious fountains.
  Our father took the whole family to the Inland Empire

    where groves were laid down in all directions
    like the careful quilting of God.
  Robber barons built their mansions

    and the fields of the Lord were planted in citrus.

Churches reared straight up and were shot
    through by boys. We spent our first vacation
  at the Sleepy Bear while our father ministered

to a fallen window and we threw ourselves over
and over in the bleached water of the pool,
hot dirty light shafting down on our heads.

Years later I went back to Riverside

and met a man who brought me to his house.
He'd been shot in the chest, a large-caliber
weapon, and when he took his shirt off,

his skin was still surprised, an epicenter
and ripples, all of it scar. I wanted
to see the exit wound, but couldn't ask.

I wanted to see the actual damage,

the way the body took it, the light in the church
when no one is there but the glazier
and his small daughter, a girl not left behind

to throw herself against the flat slap
of water, eyes rimmed red
with bleach, a plume from the steel mill

above our heads, one great chimney

called Bess towering over the blast furnace
and many coking ovens
without names, the leaves of the orange

trees in Fontana already blackened.
They harvested the last grapefruit
during the Second World War, after that

the trees couldn't give.

To go to Riverside when churches
    were stoned and men
  were shattered. I imagine my father

  on scaffolding, his careful hands,
    the way the three women were tender
  taking down the crucified Christ

    and their tenderness made the soldiers afraid.

His Burning Cloud

The year my father stops talking
the cold shrinks and learns
to glide through the grid
of fabric against my skin.
A bee drills its zero
into wood, and oleanders
smack the wind with red
bomber lips. Mother's
flying small flags of laundry
out back while Father haunts
the garage. Silence is his burning
cloud. The air is fat with poison
kisses. *Pray* she says in a ropy
voice to a full quiver of kids
perched on her bedspread. And
we do. We call on God who
holds invisible wires to
return words to his mouth.

Northridge Quake

1

Not the stopped trains,
not the ants streaming out to read
the invisible, not the way the city
struggled to restore coverage
so the camera could zoom
the crack from chimney to base,
not the marriage of fire and water
as the main and the line crumpled
together with a sudden understanding,
not the clock face that grinned
and went numb at 4:31, not the jolt
of his body thrashing up out of sleep
as the flesh of buildings fell
from architecture of bone, no,
the wooden chest is as close
as I ever get to what happened.
First a lunging, layers and
layers of thunder. And yes,
the swell of a wave, water's
surge, a girl in a wooden chest
on the rolling seas, waves
not capped or foaming, chest
drifting. Then, the dead air
of the house when it stops
humming its secret mantras
and we're the only ones left
with our little scalloped breaths.
I've broken free, I whispered
to the dead air.

2

Mother described that chest
                              many times,
each with a suave dangerous
stranger, pocket full of sweetmeats,
out there trolling
in concentric curves, all the strangers
she ever spoke of.

They all have a trunk large enough
                  to wedge in a child's body.

3

She predicted our colors
                    and postures
in those chests, a phrase like
                    cut to ribbons
in the mind's eye of our
dime store where spools of grosgrain
              with looped edges
all pulled down wildly off their spindles
and criss-crossed,
wound about the children of the May
cramped in their trunks.

After the burning and cuttings,
we might look like motley,
like bright rags, like the stamps
of foreign lands pasted
one across the other
in a hodge-podge of destinations.

And the cigarettes would be
              welcome compared to

other things.
Oh, they lit us up in a way
we could understand
         as she gestured
in the air and mimed stubbing them
                  out on child's flesh.

And then what, one of us would breathe.
They lock the chests, she'd hiss,

turning an imaginary key,

         and throw them in the LA River.

4

Our mother could cleave
to a tenet, our mother
could hold a faith.
For years we'd crane
our necks, press our faces
to the window glass, peering
down flood channels
where a trunk might snag
on a mudbar against a
stand of rushes.
Never enough flow
to carry them out,
but they must have wanted
to reach the sea by San Pedro
where the longest thoroughfares
end in cliffs and refineries,
and children can be lifted
and floated west. Never returned.
She made that clear.
But eased somehow and carried,
and I wanted that too.

5

Is there something to the stories massing in the atmosphere and the shape
of a life? The way each shock wave lifted the barge of our marriage bed
and gliding down into the trough, I knew I would have to leave him. The
video only confirmed it—rebar orphaned from its cinderblock, skeletons
left standing while fallen flesh invented itself inside the disaster. By the
first night, fever clouds had formed over the valley sifting musk on all
our heads. It's ravishing, that sense that fate is upon us.

6

What else could it be
but the workings of desire
when, after the fire turns
the hills to ash
and the sky passes
through its whiskey colors,
the rains come, rushing
down through culverts
faster than a man can run?
St. Francis Dam only needed
a small quake—concrete is supple
like skin, it suppurates, bubbles
and bursts. Something slips
inside you, nose down, the chest
slides a watery slope
just as though
          you are that child
and free because you finally
reach the sea.

I Have Not Said If I Believe

She sprang out of the pine plank table
at Nana's house, a witch with a rope
around her neck and all the havoc spilling
out encoded in our DNA. I studied
a dipping barometer and felt dirty beneath
my clothes, a bone fingered and sucked.
Mother favored gray for me, not that
it mattered a flip. Elder brother carried
our witch sewn in a vein in his thigh.
I did not think she hammered there.
They set a match to sixteen candles.
She was hanged not burnt, he announced,
pressure falling, needle notching
toward dimensions where a witch
is hanging still, her ankles stretched
longer than human, *she had six
children, her name was Lydia.* He started
the song for ha-ha. *Never been kissed*,
crooned first brother, *lost count*, cracked
the other, *sally, sally,* I muttered while
mother's mouth goes darker and
tighter. *Hurry up and blow.* Everyone
laughed when the flames died out.

That Stone

I like it out here under the barren peach tree
that flowers but cannot give. I like it

because the furnace of the wind blows hot air
at me and the birds creak from a nether tree

rusty hinge birds, and I nod along to their ruined tunes,
because I'm more here than I am there under

a poundage of failure, maybe it's all the sad things
he whispers in my ear when I'm sleeping,

at home the verbs all pine for nouns, whimpering
for agents the way the baby whimpers

all the time, that little bundle of dark water, that stone
wrapped in swaddling cloth I crouch above half-

bent and try to hush because my mother taught me
how to pass into silence with her implements,

mallet or spatula, and the great clatter of pots against
pans as the children flee, scattered to hide, hunched

with my cousin beside me behind the cinderblock
wall, *I didn't know your mother was like this*

she breathes, and I nod because what is there to say?

The Beautiful World

Our father went against our mother that day.
Because of his promise to us. This happened
years ago. The long carriage of the station
wagon hurtled along Highway 99 in August,
windows cranked down to fly-strewn dusty
fields. Madame Rosa's neon hand appeared
beside the roadway long before we could

make out the red letters: *Psychic Readings.*
And then beneath in smaller script: *Past
Present   Future.* The inner tubes were
inflated in the back because he'd promised
upcanyon there'd be a stop. It started
there in that promise—waiting for the river.
In the little knot of that promise it all began,

the station wagon rolling across seams
in the bridge over the Kings River and the
children clamoring for water. I never said
what I wanted, but for a moment I wanted
to step inside Madame Rosa's house, to see
beyond the parlor into the kitchen where she
might stand when there were no customers,

staring maybe at the cottonwood that line
the riverbank or the dotted Swiss of her curtains,
not thinking exactly, just letting her mind run,
but the children begged for water
and our father pulled off the road. Our mother
saw the barbed wire and the sign that said *Private
Property.* She saw doom everywhere and said so.

It was not our way to break the law, to trespass
onto farmlands, fields left fallow in long

grass with channels of the Kings cutting through,
marked by tiny canopies of scrub willow which
always mean water. We stopped in spite of
our mother and all of us went against her. Madame
Rosa was impossible because strangers were not allowed

to touch us, we must not open our hands to them,
fingers spidering, palms moist in the lines they would trace,
heart line, fate line. I never believed I would die then.
Madame Rosa was out of the question.
That was not our way. My mind likes impossible
thoughts, likes to hold the barbed wire wide
and slide carefully through.

I held the wire for them all, led them through
the razor grass to the soggy banks.
Our mother sat silent about breaking the law
in a hot car on a seething day while we entered
the bower of the river and were permitted
one by one to launch ourselves.
It's all green light inside the river-chamber,

the water moss-brown, a little more persistent
than we expected. We were happy
at first, talking, negotiating the snags, calling
back and forth, and then happy quietly
because our father had given in,
our mother had been bested, overruled,
and that's unseemly to speak of,

yet joyous, the heart drowning in joy,
the way love must be, as the world
goes greener and all the trees kneel down,
sweeping their long arms down in greenness,
light shafted wafer-thin, filtered bottle-green,
water persistent—oh, the water
was going somewhere; it had a destination

which meant so did we, because all do.
Madame Rosa can see this, each with a destiny
and an end, though we only thought then
of the beautiful world, our hands open,
the lines rippling across like water, we were going
where the river was going, maybe the green room
where the fairies live at the base of the rushes.

That seemed true because the channel was twisting
smaller, we too might be shrinking to match
this narrow space, as small as any one of us
ever wanted to be, and up ahead, there was
something in the water, a snag, or a rock.
Something I came up against and tried to push off.
When I pushed it was spongy, not sharp

and anchored like a rock, not twisted like limbs
or branches, spongy and huge, blocking the channel,
not knowing, I pushed again, and this *thing*,
not sprung free, not dislodged,
but *a vastness floating*, lifted up, and I touched
thin hair and bone, extension and bloat, lank
wet hide, I touched death,

the current was pushing me, pushing
my body against the hide, and I saw the head suddenly,
the dead head with its open eyes and doe ears
on the great body, sprawled legs snagged
and held in place, a cow that had wandered into the stream
and drowned, held now where I was held up against her.
A cow who had come down to the banks for the last time

and light poured through the willows and beat its wings
in the poplars and maybe she lifted her head, hooves in the mire,
and saw what I saw, light passing through spires
of reeds, her life running into the river, at first
without knowledge, and then knowing. Silence

and then sound. A voice coming from a tin box
shouting, *a dead cow, a dead cow,*

so that we would not all come to this place,
one child after another boxed in and wedged
up against the wall of floating death
with her dark-water eyes. How small her head
beneath the water, but her body had grown in death
and I couldn't get around it.
So I had to slide into the water and

push against her swimming for the side.
I'm not allowed to touch death.
My hands paddled against the stomach wall
of the creature, against slickness, the spongy
way it gave, and yet held me. Death is not quiet.
Madame Rosa knows this. You can hear it
when you stop your thrashing.

A sound will come then, a kind of crooning
rising from the water, brown as blood, a song like oil,
insinuating. We were promised water.
The children clamored. That summer
we went into the river the day was seething.
The water promised one thing, our mother another.
I kicked away from the slippery hide

hoping everything was held inside,
but it wasn't. Death was leaching
out, oozing onto me. Stumbling finally
to shore, the others did not even tease me
because they saw I was covered in death,
that I had to walk that way back to our mother,
and for an instant she would be glad.

Sarabande

I never look for stars here. They pale
next to LA's green unearthly glow spreading sixty miles.

My father, I don't think of him when I think of stars,
distant and cold. He sang, *Don't let the stars get in your eyes,*

don't let the moon break your heart,
then a long Perry Como trope ending with *for you're the only one I'll
ever love.*

Fast falls the eventide, wind feathers the artemisia,
silken and murmurous as tropical grammar.

Now darkness moves slowly through him with seasons, occasions,
like sarabande, that courtly dance of the 17ᵗʰ century—

of Cancer it is written, *a body black and without eyes,*
and of sarabande, *a grave melody expressing no passion*

other than ambition. I don't think of stars here,
that starry night unfurls somewhere further out

on the other side of the Transverse Range, where Cancer's
visible to the salt-ringed eye, the beehive cluster pulsing,

her weak oil lamps hanging over us all.

Her Breath Comes in Feathers

The universe is made of stories,
not of atoms.
        —Muriel Rukeyser

I sit here from morning until evening
while liquids drip into my mother's
body through what they call a port,
an opening they carved because
her veins are soft. Hanging from
a crane, four bags dock into her,
one for hunger, two for hurt,
the third for *c. difficile*, and blood
to wage her battle. They drip and I sit.

Read to Mom, my sister tells me,
she still enjoys animal stories.
So I bring a children's book,
Balto, bravest dog ever, who
saved the entire town of Nome
from diphtheria, and nobody
had to die. *Do you want to hear*
this story? Move your hand,
Mom, raise your fingers a little.
She doesn't move.

Are stories beside the point now?
Do you want to hear about Dad?
I'll tell you what he's doing.
She doesn't move. *He's smashing*
cans. He smashes them with
a sledgehammer and puts them
in bags and takes them to recycle.
Nobody can fit more cans in a bag
than Dad. No one gets them flatter.

There's no sound or movement,
but there is, I think, a quality
of attention. We all believe
what we want to believe.
She's not moving her hand,
but still, I think she's listening.

Coyote Song

Inside the night, this hospital, asylum,
this party for those undone by desire, forever
unslaked, inside a house inside the night,
I'm inside

this house with eight beams and moonlight
pulling on the past through skylights, this house
of white noise, wind and dry heat, lonely
house on a ridge line, house of ordinary
shame,

my sister's house with corrals and outbuildings
around it, and beyond that, the dog
patrolling, and beyond that, skirts and folds
of the mountain rising in rumpled geologic
scrolls into the range.

At the center
beneath the moon's silence that nothing
ever changes, muffled in blankets with fear
beside me on my little bench of sleep,
I can hear their voices,

could be three or twenty-three,
unhinged saints gabbling to their shadows,
or panty-sniffers, drug-trippers in all flavors
past vanilla, could be Birnam wood
on the move, the shriek of its roots thirsty
and air-bruised, or a pack of lunatics
crooning norteño songs.

What is certain is *advent.*
They're coming down,
                coming towards

the heart beneath the feathers,
coming for
what can't be protected,
on a beam of dread,
riding that ray.

I'm listening, my eyes snapped-open
inside darkness, other people in other rooms
who know how to sleep through a night
like this night, thrown against the roundness
of the world which is desire.

The old bitch guards this night on the ranch,
half shepherd, half other, this is her watch,
she gallops the perimeter, anxious to sound like
more than one dog, though she's going arthritic
and her paws strike hard ground.

Now they quiet, penitents, lunatics,
marauders and ragpickers, *quiet.*
Only one left behind and the moon
            is his hieroglyph,
one creature padding
        down the mountain,
coming closer.

Coyote knows a good joke,
he only wants to let her in on it.
He can't stop laughing, can't stop
crying, can't stop licking the crevices
clean, licking *safety* and *duty*
until they're empty.

I hear the dog listening, ears lifted.
Coyote's tongue slides into night
air, pressing narcotic vowels through
wonder, through *longing*

and longing and wonder awaken. She's close
to that edge, that border in the night
where one thing becomes another and even
an old dog who's worked a ranch eleven years
feels the urge to let loose, blow this little
settlement, *go wild.*

Clouds loose and blue in the arms
of the moon, slant light on this mountain raking
us, the dog and I, we feel the pull. Imagine
a woman trying to come between
coyote and the female he's after
when she knows

what is dark and offers itself and vanishes
has come for her at last? The body wants
what it can't have, to follow the path
of thirst through the rent in the wire
beyond the corral.

The dog doesn't move, but who knows
better than she the small outpost
death has set up in her, maybe she's all
desire now to slip under the moon
and chase down that lure.

Coyote wheedles and croons another minute
or two, then lopes off, calling over his shoulder
in a language even I can understand,
the right names for things
not kept in heaven.

Wildfire at Witch Creek

The roof floated away, beams disappeared
and thousands of ten-penny nails dropped

 plumb into black. Most of the trees survived
though some had their hearts burnt out

 and didn't know they died in that storm
made of heat and wind and revisioning rain—

 now ash droplets and chalk and fine-grain
drifting sand filling arroyos smooth

 out the land as gently as my sister did, smearing
salve in her horses' blasted eyes.

 The palo verde by her door grew from stones
and did not pass away, but ruin

 is not a wall, more like a hand with many fingers
reaching through the pines to grasp the house.

 When she went back to the rubble, sifting
in screens for our mother's wedding ring,

 she already knew its small run of brilliance
had done.

Under the Lemon Tree

Not rain, but fine mist
falls from my lemon tree,
a balm of droplets in green shadow.

Six years now my mother gone to earth.
This dew, light as footsteps of the dead.
She often walked out here, craned her neck,
considered the fruit, hundreds of globes
in their leathery hides, figuring on
custard and pudding, meringue and
hollandaise.

But her plans didn't work out.

The tree goes on unceasingly—lemons fall
and fold into earth and begin again—
me, I come here as a salve against heat,
come to languish, to let the soft bursts—
essence of citrus, summer's distillate—
drift into my face and settle. Water and gold
brew in the quiet deeps at the far end
of the season. Leaves swallow the body
of light and the breath of water brims over.

My hands cup each other the way hers did.

To the Unborn Child

Already almost April, your birth month,
nine new moons since sockeye salmon
sluiced up the Talkeetna, since the great sow
lumbered into the river, cubs trailing her,

since a man knelt and dipped his paw
into the icy rush, and with one swipe
became your father. Now we set flowers
and twigs in your mother's hair, rub

her feet with scented oil, brew blackberry
tea, pots of it, as much as she wants—
she is suffused with you, child, and
you are full of everything that made you—

the nebula that lofted up your molecules,
the high place hidden in clouds, shifting light,
cotton grass, blood and bone and amber,
the love that set you swimming . . .

Homesteader

for Caleaf at 8 weeks

But the light finds you, traveler

> and the morning's
> smudged thumbprint
> gives way

> spokes' sheen
> almost green
> wickered through limbs

The light finds you, homesteader

> her side-stare
> on your dark hair
> where silk unspools its spiral

Let's haul our bodies like seals
let the sun slump over us

Let's haul our bodies onto shoals
let the blue-skeined sun slump down over us

Did you hear what *la Mexicana* on Front Street was saying?

Precious feather, little grandfather, milky stone—
is all this old to you, or still unknown?

Here Day Is Surrounded

by night & my datura
blooms again in spite of punishing winds
pale locoweed filled with milky poison,
persisting even though light diminishes
and must we shrink to fit this new harshness?
Still eighteen hours until I see you. The wind
circles this house and moves on. The house
turns away from the light. I put a rectangle
of dark chocolate on my tongue and called you
because I couldn't wait, got the machine,
your cool voice, all your beautiful
indifference.

THREE

This Time

Consider the sun.
Let one photon struggling through plasma
for millions of years toward the surface

be the journey of the soul.

She enters the convection zone in the morning, rising
and falling on currents of heat, takes a room
facing south, on the highest floor.

She's on the balcony contemplating
the journey, eyes locked on radiance,
a procession of clouds domed like mosques.

Is it forbidden before you leap
to tell the secrets of your prison-house?

What would the truth have been?

I too have harmed myself in the furnace,
the viscera where atoms split apart.

From the surface
it's a quick passage, only seven minutes
to stream 93 million miles.

This time, let her body open
enough to receive that one particle of joy.

Anna Mae

Anyone from the river valley knows the signs
posted at the docks and on the banks *Do Not Consume,*

and the black icon, no fish in particular,
but the shadow of all fish.

You remember those signs but maybe not Anna Mae.
She lived in the valley all her life,

when she was young people looked at her,
her freckled arms and fair skin,

slight, but what guys called "stacked,"
a real head-turner with light serious eyes.

She worked at the GE plant on the river bluffs
where everyone in town worked

at some point, but she stuck with it and they promoted her
to lead lady in the pouring room.

By then, she was no knockout, past beauty,
just something to know about her and for us girls to ponder.

Those were the days when they used PCBs
in everything from radios to guided missiles

and GE dumped the tailings in the river.
Only young women worked the pouring room,

I don't know why, and Anna Mae worked the cauldron,
controlled the thickness and pace

of the solution, well, she was lead lady for a reason,
always steady, no one flighty could keep the line going

the way she did. One time the chemists came down
to watch and I heard one of them say, *This shit is gold,*

so excited because they developed the mixture themselves.
After that one girl would turn to the next

and say *this shit is gold* with an edge, and we laughed
and played looks-like/smells-like at break—

like amber, like hardpan, like honey, like gasoline,
like cloves with steel shavings mixed in,

and once Anna Mae lifted her head and said,
like a mouthful of coins, close enough

to taste with each breath as she bent to control
the speed. Anna Mae died a long time ago—

goblin molecules rode into her blood.
She turned yellow, but worked

almost up to the last, and then Phyllis took over.
Anna's big gray husband came in and faced us

and for once they let the line stop. *Anna Mae loved*
all you girls like her own, because we couldn't have . . . none.

We bowed our heads until Phyllis turned the machine back on.
Now all these years later I remember Anna Mae

when I walk past those signs down by the river.
Fish circle slowly in the dark musculature of the water—

drifting close to the surface
as if they could swim into air and be healed.

Antidote for Night

So much as close my eyes
and a flayed Labrador is laid at my doorstep.

And here's the same bone
lodged in the slippery pottage
of my heart

where this man croons, *Baby you're so sweet*
until I take his head between my hands
and lay it on my breast.

There's the moon in the high window, her wall-eye
glancing off me, and a few bobbing stars,
every tawdry shining thing.

I've identified Venus more times
than I can count as an agent for insomnia,
a broad sail that catches the wind and slides away.

Not even halfway through the hours,
his fitful sleep, wheeze of a saber-saw,
waves receding on a rocky shore,

breath whip-snaking down a chute, until his body
forgets—how still, how close the kingdom,
one stalled-gulp away,

and I jostle his dying shoulder—he recoils, yes,
rebels, back now, mouth full of silver,
What? he moans to darkness, *what?*

Whistle Keeps on Blowing

Then there's the time four trumpet players came in together
after hours at the Happy Rhone Club in Harlem
where Armstrong was playing the new hot music.

They meant to cut him and thought it might take
four to do it, spelling each other to wear him down.
It must have been something so new,

so brilliant, floating in the air like the hand
of Apollo on the panpipe, on the lyre, and the ripple
into being when air opens and a form is born, a four-beat

pulse under a two-beat rag, the piano player slapping his foot
on the hard wooden floor in a brothel in Storyville
and the quarter notes and pairs of eighths create a

rocking motion which begets a pulse which begets *hot*
which jazzes it, and it starts to swing.
You can almost see it that way—in the beginning

the pipe-playing Marsyas perched on a rock
and the first elemental sound, the *ya ya ya* pearling down
through the panpipe and maybe a fragment of prayer

because he must have known it couldn't derive only
from him *Thou art air / Thou art the void, O Lord,*
and beside him, the god of light, face bent over the music,

and no hint of the horror to come because who ever imagines
the horror to come, the body swollen with fluid,
a catheter threaded through an artery directly into the heart,

tiny shoes beside huge ankles and feet. No, this is a pastoral
scene, a moment when they can believe,
almost a romance, with nymphs ranged behind the trees

and anyone can see the truth: a rush of breath
on the face of water animated it all, and don't we believe
in this idyll, the little freshets of color that flare

before the darkening in the sky, the high-rise by the waterside
opaque long before nightfall, and if you don't believe
you can look in the Bible, here in the front

a special section: *Where to Find It: A Remedy for the Blues*
or *Spiritual Blackout,* thumbing through to *The Song of Songs,*
which is as close as it gets to the landscape of

the Golden Age spread out behind Marsyas, receding to rose-gray.
Sadness needs a setting, for instance any garden—
it's all birdsong out there in the spicy bitter verdure,

the trill, the throat-fill, air heated up in their tiny chambers
and hurled out repeating *Thou art fair, thou art fair,*
their song is regret, the last ache in the wound of Paradise,

though why would anyone believe Louis Armstrong
ever regretted his time sentenced to the Waif's Home for Boys
and there, one day, handed the first cornet, learning fast,

till he was the one blowing a call for just about everything
they did—for soup, for baths, for awakening. So
nothing is not breath—a voice rasping from inside the juke

on Perdido Street: *Whistle keeps on blowing and I got my debts
to pay,* the boys in knickers and black stockings marching in step
through the mud streets of Storyville carrying banged-up instruments

and the only variable is time, that instant when he knew to take
something simple, declarative and golden, and flatten it a little,
let it vibrate out through the end. And if it feels like it will never end—

and inexplicable, the way you can't get past a certain truth,
no matter how often you turn it, you're still up against a self
that never wanted to come into being, not on those terms, not

coming from that past. Life is no Absolute good. And still we
want to live. He never backed down; he rose up, they said,
like an offended lion. When he got angry he could really play,

while the four sat back and he let go—*This is how it's done, boys*—
the first wobbling notes, valved longing, a woman leaning into a man,
held up only by music, breath joined in huge arcs passing through

this pure cylinder starting with emptiness. Nobody could cut him.
It's not the tune that matters, it's the way you play it.
You can play it for laughs when it isn't funny,

so when they asked, *What do you believe in?* he answered,
Nothing, so I guess you got nothing to disabuse me of, the wheel turning
the way he turned it, loose, springy, even brash,

turning a phrase *I got my debts to pay* into a clear exposition
of the world as it is with its flattened thirds and sevenths
and what if he believed even when he acted otherwise,

believed when he refused to answer, the god long-muscled,
his face bent over the music, and by this time the nymphs
had moved closer, were playing the part of butchers,

one stripping the skin away like plastic wrap, another holding
a propane torch while a Renaissance dog lapped the blood,
and the question put: *you'd do anything to stay alive, wouldn't you?*

and hush, the measure of silence, because there's room inside
a measure for affirmation and denial. The doctor said
they'd agreed to "compromise," nothing else mattered

but to go on playing. Sometimes he came to that place
where he saw what the music saw and he was the music,
and then the music went on and saw more,

so what could it mean, this heart, with its *de dum, de dum,*
Wah shoo shoo wah, that would stop the beat?
It don't mean a thing; a pause, then swaying a little,

the beautiful attack, horn straying only slightly from melody,
that first element, a rush of breath in the mouth
of water, *I got a mind to leave this world /*

and I got a mind to stay

Say Nothing

Whatever I want the world will take away from me . . . I thought about it that way—stake out boundaries, build walls, don't trumpet good fortune in white rooms. Don't put "true love" out there as a proposition. Fate adores sending a rogue wave to capsize your little skiff just when the weather seems cloudless. *Cuidado,* my *comadre* used to say to me, *the Lady* might drop by—you could get *la visita,* if you don't watch out.

My strategy? *Say nothing.*

So I never dared be the moon to his sun, my scarred white stone to his fire, no, we were both wordless, in the drink—though water's not mute, but conversational, the murmur of water's ordinary—a husband driving home from work turning onto his own street just as the light goes watery violet, and the gurgle, the steady slap of the heart is water, that elaborate pump I listen to, my ear curved against his breastbone and inside a liquid fist clenches and opens. My sister once hired a dowser for a barren plot she owned on the edge of the Sonora, and oh how the willow bucked and quivered in his hands diving for the hidden spring, a branch machete-struck from its limb tough enough to remember, even severed, soft enough to sob for water, one body to another, what's between them at sea, the wordless drift of interior currents, our two bodies only rarely glinting their tie-dyed silks of water, all that wet splendor—*should I be saying this?*

Another Dream of Death

as simple as two ring-necked doves
in a winter-bare tree, so close they're clearly a pair,
one flaps away, the other shivers
her feathers and hunkers down on the branch—
after a time she goes too. Or maybe it's a wound
to my skull, not a bullet, but a shaft struck
down into greasy wet darkness where women
surround me, the *King's women* I call them,
who urge without words towards something
final and visceral, what—I don't know. And once
a blonde crawled toward me under a table
and ravished me with her lip-stick red mouth,
but still every morning I refuse,
and walk away into daylight.

Something Fresh

This is my chance to untangle the riddle—he's a bramble, an enigma, a dew-eyed ramble, mouth full of quips, both the bird and the bush, brother and briar, a metabolic frolic. An off-kilter wallop. Able to pound out, scratch out, peck out—he's no tabula rasa, he's written up, written off into thousands of sunsets, black and white and red all over. He's the noisiest quiet you'll ever want to know, my big yes, my full court press, chary, a skinflint with lexicon, but rash on syntax; no warrior, yet nature built him compact—*the better to swing a battle-axe*—he told me *that* on our second date—a stray molecule yearning to burn in the bonds of delight, he's my snake-bit baby, my history of the blues, my personal fuse-box, my litmus test, my witness, a stroll in a dog-park, no saint, but, yeah, the guy is *something fresh about a bird . . .*

Crossing Over

This time of year I like the gnarled
     little sugar skulls
like dolled-up potatoes,
fingerlings with eyes gouged out,
    daisies growing through the sockets,

this time of year always wondering
              about that baby I lost,
otherwise don't look back,
otherwise why think at all?

When my body refused, his presence
didn't dissipate right away,
never meant any harm,
just trailing after in the ether

and now this ether-light's *shining*
        and the wind twitches,
I can hear the ropes bite the macadam,
  crossing over,

neighbor girls playing Double Dutch,
     chanting as they jump
but can't make out their faces in the glare.
Their ropes strike the ground in rhythm.

When my baby girl was born
sometimes she took it so hard just living,
I crooned *don't come undone now, don't come undone*
the way my grandma used to.

She raised prodigious chickens
     out back,
great-breasted matrons

who laid huge eggs,
most every one had two yolks
and whenever one of us asked
How'd they do it?

she answered *they're double-souled,*
honey.

This time of year, gold lingers
in thin autumn air
ether-light shining
crossing over

ropes beat the ground in rhythm
I can hear their voices
but can't make out their faces.

Black Hands

I wept when the rains came so soon,
  knowing how he hated to get his feet
wet—now wrapped in a pillowcase
   in the cold ground. I wept on the question
of his sleep, the vet closed his eyes, first
  the milky blind one, and then the one
  he used for pleading. He gave
   a small final mew when the air left,
and his dark muzzle relaxed—she cupped
   her hand beneath that last sound and
closed his jaw, dark face, dark paws,
  ivory and seal, his old dustbag of a body
  abandoned at last. We swaddled him
  like an infant. Since he's been gone
every afternoon a tightening in my throat
   takes me out past the crumbling incinerator
  past the empty hutches, wood blanched
silver by the wind, rusted screens sprung
  free, back into the sphere of the lemon, unshaped
  so many seasons now, its crown a bramble
  of dead branches. Too much fruit kills the life
at the tip of the bough, darkness sets into
   the fingers, *black hands* my daughter calls
them, the tallow won't reach, no,
  it's flowing into misshapen lanterns
  glowing sulfur yellow in the tangle
  and thorn. And everywhere the smell
of waxy blossoms, faintly bitter zest
  of dew, the whole tree exhaling not just
perfume, but breath of leafmold and
  compost—he used to stretch out
  like feline Egypt in its aura. Late
  afternoon, green air almost cold, and
the black hands strain upward, reaching

towards that indigo in the dome,
trying to wash themselves clean, my life
   come to this disturbed earth in the shadow
   where cowslips grow, shade-lovers—
my cowslips—like me, paper white,
   simpletons my daughter says,
as if it's vulgar to crave to be
   first in your loose lacy whorls—
crowding cyclamen on the mound,
   five petals drawn together
   like the clasp on a lady's handbag,
and the color, cherry cider, but she says, *no,*
   darker, more like the hammered
seeds inside a pomegranate, and suddenly
   I want to be simple as cyclamen—
   pale horseshoe on its split leaf—
   a stretched heart—and underground, his small
body hollowing out a chamber . . .

First Storm

For Caleaf at 16 weeks

Rain falling in soft
cadence under the juniper
drops filling, tipping
rolling off branches
in dollops so cold they burn.
He is any small animal
a kit, a coyote pup,
leaning into weather
solemn, deep in his senses—
the chief inlets of Soul
Blake tells us,
and is he all soul
or all body?
No concern of his.
He presses away
from my arms. No idea,
but in green gray
shadow, archipelagos
of black water
on asphalt,
dark wet shining.
His hand goes out,
cupped for the raindrop
in this first storm
of the world

How to Go On

Begin with forgetting, extinguish desire,
practice not wanting for half an hour
every morning, practice forgetting
the hand cradled under the nape
of your neck, mouth to your mouth's kiss,
but remember, no matter what you do, one
desire will remain. Hunger is the first and
last word. When all words in California
slide into the sea, hunger will be the last
to fall. Should they all plunge out of the sky
in flames, hunger burns the brightest.
This is what you must do: go buy some
yellow stick, don't bother with butter
or margarine, yellow stick will do, nothing
comes cheaper by the pound and it melts.
That's the point. Buy a yam. This will cost
thirty-seven cents which you can find at
the bottom of your purse or under your couch.

Pay attention to the name of the yam—
red jewel or ruby or red garnet. Sometimes
the ad names the land of its origin. If you
don't know, imagine this place, say, Livingston,
California, on a floodplain. Imagine the soil,
sandy or clay, porous or heavy, and the yams
underneath reaching for each other, the erotic
longing of tuber for tuber. This feeds you also.
Heat the oven. Warmth is a kind of food.
While it's cooking, stroke your chest along
the bony ridge of the breastplate down to the
wishbone. Stand by the heat. When the yam
is ready, it splits open on its own. Wait until
the sugar begins to burn on the oven wall.
Then it's perfect. Let the yellow stick slide
into a pool. This waiting can nourish you.

Now eat it in small bites, vermilion on a cold
night. In between bites, say *it's enough*.

Imagine the yam is hungry for the inside
of you. Close your eyes. Picture yourself
clothed in red silk. You can eat the winter
night, dissolve it into the yam to a perfect
temperature. Imagine a volcano throws
out a vein of hot water at one-hundred-
eighty degrees from the side of a mountain.
These springs belong to you. Imagine the wind
is blowing and you are not cold because the wind
belongs to you. Imagine you are standing in a mine
full of rubies and each gem licking along the length
of the dark vein warms you. Imagine all this
dissolved into the yam which is yours. It will be
enough. But be careful, if you do it too often, any
one who sets out food will be able to tame you.

Murmur

Right now it's simple—*agua de tamarindo,*
a marmalade cat straggling across the street at twilight,
her solemn eyes on me, ditching dinner for melted
Cabot cheddar on seed bread, hunks of papaya, rose-tinged
flesh mounded in a blue glass bowl, black coffee
with a bitter undertow, the world has not stopped speaking,
all manner of things murmur—*nothing here means*
you harm, the way elliptical shapes of light fall
at just the right angle between beams of the *ramada,*
moving shadows the wind guides through this mottled
world, cloudshadow feathering my shoulders, leaf patterns
stirring, and—just like that—the wind leaves me whole,
easy to say yes to the monsoon sliding up from Mexico
in a musky velvet gown, *gracias* to the small rivers of air
off the ocean that flow up dry creekbeds every afternoon—
it all comes down to air, to the bargain a stranger made
a long time ago with a dying girl when he turned
her head and cleared the passage so she could breathe
fully the accident of happiness, billows of air
taken in, given back, and—it's a snap—breathing
like a champ, like I loved my own lost self all along.

Acknowledgments

I am thankful to the editors of the following publications for their encouragement, and for giving these poems a home, sometimes in earlier incarnations:

ARTLIFE: "Another Woman," "Coyote Song," "What It Takes";
Barrow Street: "The Beautiful World";
Café Solo: "I Have Not Said If I Believe";
Chaparral: "Chinese Lantern";
Crying Sky: "Northridge Quake," "That Stone";
Levure Litteraire: "Another Dream of Death";
Los Angeles Review: "Nobody Knows";
Miramar: "Antidote for Night," "Black Hands," "Murmur," "Once,"
     "Possum," "Sarabande," "Say Nothing," "Under the Lemon Tree";
Packinghouse Review: "Viento";
Solo: "Whistle Keeps on Blowing";
Solo Café: "Her Breath Comes in Feathers," "Sanchez";
Solo Novo: "Crossing Over," "Same Loom";
Ten California Poets: "How to Go On";
The Kerf: "Here Day Is Surrounded";
Ventura Life: "His Burning Cloud";
Wide Awake: Poets of Los Angeles and Beyond: "To Go to Riverside."

To Phil Taggart, *gracias por vida*.

I am grateful to Beyond Baroque, and the poetry communities of Southern California and the Central Coast for enabling me to walk into any room where they gather, to the City of Ventura for Individual Artist Grants, to Deena Metzger for her heart-opening work, to Herbert Scott—always, and to New Issues Press which he brought into being, to the Vermont College community of writers, especially my teachers, Nancy Eimers, Cynthia Huntington, William Olsen, Betsy Sholl, and David Wojahn, for compassion, for brilliance.

Particular thanks for encouragement and support to Ron Alexander, Polly Bee, Christopher Buckley, James Cushing, Carol Davis, ellen, Paul Fericano, Friday, Elijah Imlay, Wayne Lindberg, Perie Longo, Suzanne Lummis, Glenna Luschei, Sarah Maclay, Holaday Mason, Ines Monguio, Richard Newsham, Nereyda de la O, Enid Osborn, Anita Pulier, John Ridland, Lin Rolens, Mary Kay Rummel, Fernando Salinas, Shelley Savren, Bruce Schmidt, Dian Sousa, Barry Spacks, David St. John, David Starkey, Kevin Patrick and Patti Sullivan, Amy Uyematsu, Doris Vernon, Florence Weinberger, Hilda Weiss, Jackson Wheeler, Paul Willis, Chryss Yost, Kim Young, Mariano Zaro . . . and Summer Women and the Bookish Ladies. Gratitude to the artist, Fiona Lee MacLean, and the entire community of Exploring New Horizons. Thanks to Peter Conners, Jenna Fisher, Melissa Hall, Sandy Knight, and BOA Editions for your kindness and hard work. Maia, without you, there would be no poetry. Laure-Anne Bosselaar, you are a gift in my life.

Gratitude and love to my crazy, darling family.

About the Author

Marsha de la O was born and raised in Southern California. Both sides of her family arrived in the Los Angeles area before William Mulholland built the aqueduct that brought in water from the eastern Sierras. De la O worked as a bilingual teacher in Los Angeles and the rural community of Santa Paula for more than twenty-five years. She holds a Master of Fine Arts degree from Vermont College. Her first book, *Black Hope,* was awarded the New Issues Press Poetry Prize. She lives in Ventura, California, with her husband, poet and editor Phil Taggart. Together, they produce poetry readings and events in Ventura County and are also the editors and publishers of the literary journal *Askew.*

BOA Editions, Ltd.
American Poets Continuum Series

Colophon

The Isabella Gardner Poetry Award is given biennially to a poet in mid-career with a new book of exceptional merit. Poet, actress, and associate editor of *Poetry* magazine, Isabella Gardner (1915–1981) published five celebrated collections of poetry, was three times nominated for the National Book Award, and was the first recipient of the New York State Walt Whitman Citation of Merit for Poetry. She championed the work of young and gifted poets, helping many of them to find publication.

The publication of this book is made possible, in part, by the special support of the following individuals:

Anonymous x 2
Nin Andrews
Nelson Adrian Blish
Susan Burke & Bill Leonardi, *in honor of Boo Poulin*
Bernadette Catalana, *in memory of Richard Calabrese*
Anne C. Coon & Craig J. Zicari
Jonathan Everitt
Gouvernet Arts Fund
Michael Hall
Jack & Gail Langerak
Barbara & John Lovenheim
Richard Margolis & Sherry Phillips
Boo Poulin, *in honor of Susan Burke & Bill Leonardi*
Deborah Ronnen & Sherman Levey
Steven O. Russell & Phyllis Rifkin-Russell